The Little Big Small Business Book

Micah Fraim

Contents

Introduction – How to Avoid Troublesome "Kelp"

"Sometimes I have a difficulty talking to people who don't race sailboats." – Bruno Gianelli

That was one of my favorite lines from *The West Wing*, a show where the dialogue was so good and the characters so unbelievably quick-witted that it made you feel like an idiot. In the scene, President Bartlet was upset that campaign advisor Bruno Gianelli was polling about something the President considered to be irrelevant. With Barlet understandably confused at the above statement, Bruno explained:

"I have difficulty sometimes talking to people who don't race sailboats. When I was a teenager, I crewed Larchmont to Nassau on a 58-foot sloop called Cantice. There was a little piece of kelp that was stuck to the hull, and even though it was little, you don't want anything stuck to the hull. So, I take a boat hook on a pole and I stick it in the water and I try to get the kelp off, when seven guys start screaming at me, right? 'Cause now the pole is causing more drag than the kelp was. See, what you gotta do is you gotta drop it in and let the water lift it out in a windmill motion. Drop it in, and let the water take it by the kelp and lift it out. In, and out. In, and out, till you got it. […] If you think that I'm going to miss even one opportunity to pick up half-a-mile boat speed, you're

*absolutely out of your mind. When it costs us nothing, when we give up **nothing**! You're out of your mind."*

The purpose of this book is just that – to help you identify potential "kelp" in your business and remove it. Through my years of advisory work as a CPA I've been able to identify some consistent areas of problems and opportunities for small businesses. These articles will be split into three basic categories:

1. Accounting, Tax, & Finance
2. Marketing & Branding
3. Valuable Miscellany (good stuff for which I couldn't find a specific category)

Some of these chapters deal with broad, very important, "mission critical" areas while others focus on more specialized or point-specific topics. Some sections of this book are interrelated and even overlap at times, while others stand in complete isolation. And perhaps you will find that certain matters that are discussed do not specifically apply to your business. However I am confident that there is information here that will resonate with you, and not just that but will work to make meaningful – and profitable – changes in your business plan. And if we aren't willing to examine every aspect of our business when it costs us **nothing**, when we give up **nothing** – well, as Bruno said, we're out of our minds.

Section 1: Accounting, Tax, & Finance

Chapter 1: To "C" or not to "C"? What Type of Corporation Should I Choose For My Business?

Most businesses eventually choose to incorporate in some form or fashion. This can have a number of benefits, both from a legal and a tax standpoint. However, the <u>type of corporate structure</u> – that is, which form of corporate entity to utilize – is one of the single most important planning decisions a business can make, and it is consistently one of the areas where I see the most misinformation given and mistakes made. Here are three examples of things I encountered all within a single month of each other:

- A small, single owner company set up as a C-Corporation
- A business with $100k in profit operating as an LLC/being taxed as a partnership
- A small business with $5k in profit that had been advised to become an S-Corporation for the "tax savings"

In each of these instances, a mistake in formation structure was made. Somebody somewhere gave the business owner bad advice – or perhaps no professional advice was sought. What is the issue with each of these examples? Let's take a closer look at the advantages and disadvantages of each of these entity types.

C-Corp

Wal-Mart, IBM, and other major corporations are C-Corporations. This is because business with: 1) more than one class of stock or 2) more than 100 shareholders are not given the option of S-Corp election. What are the benefits?

The stock is able to be widely (in the above examples, publicly) traded. This makes raising capital much easier and also makes the ownership readily transferrable. It allows for different classes of stock, which plays a major role when corporate decisions are at stake.

But the disadvantage to a C-Corp is severe. The corporation itself is taxed and then any earnings that are disbursed to shareholders – as dividends for example – are also taxed. In effect, double taxation. As small business owners, there are a select few circumstances that would warrant taking this tax hit. The above example (small company, one owner) was not one of them.

LLC

LLCs are probably one of the most popular entities for small business owners – and with good reason:

- They are easy to form
- They give the owner the benefit of limited legal liability (as do the other entities)

- If there is only one owner, they can be treated as a "disregarded entity". This means they do not require a separate tax return and all income can be done on Schedule C of the 1040. This saves money on tax preparation and is an easier process

I actually like LLCs. There are a lot of circumstances where they are the most advisable approach. But they have one major disadvantage:

- As a default, all of the earnings are considered self-employment income and are thereby subject to self-employment tax

I will go in more detail in the next section to explain why this can be an issue.

S-Corp

When possible and under the right circumstances, S-Corps are the "crème de la crème" of tax entities. They offer the same legal protection as the other entities but have one major advantage:

- Earnings in excess of the shareholder's salary are not subject to self-employment tax

Please note: _this is a discussion from a **tax** standpoint. It is possible to form an LLC or other corporate structure and elect S-Corp status for taxation purposes. **In fact**, I am actually in favor of LLCs over Incs in most cases for the **legal** setup, just not_ *necessarily the tax setup.* Let me use the second example above to illustrate. Assume that this person met the IRS qualifications for an S-Corp (and that they truly were an employee of the corporation and not using it to shield income), a reasonable salary for the profession/industry/area was determined to be $50,000, but the company made an additional $50,000 in profit. The self-employment tax is 15.3% (up until the point that you hit the Social Security cap). In this example, this is the difference in tax savings with an LLC (that has not elected S-Corp status) vs. an S-Corp:

	Income Subject to SE Tax	SE Rate	SE Tax Due
LLC	$100,000	15.30%	$15,300
S-Corp	$50,000	15.30%	$7,650

That's a savings of $7,650, not in taxable income, but in **actual tax** to be paid! All from the correct entity choice and categorization of income.

That said, S-Corps are not ideal for everyone. Look at the third example above. The $5,000 business owner could not give himself reasonable salary of $500 and then take the rest as dividends. Every penny of it was subject to SE tax. In fact, it likely cost him extra money because an additional tax return had to be filed for the S-Corp and payroll processing is now required. All in the name of "tax savings" that did not exist.

There is an old joke that if you ask an accountant any question, regardless of how rudimentary it may seem, he will always answer with "it depends". There is a lot of truth in that. Every situation I run into is different. Every client has a unique set of needs, goals, and circumstances. The right course of action for nine clients would be wrong for the tenth.

This decision is important enough and the tax ramifications potentially large enough that consulting a tax professional is likely a good investment. If you are not inclined to do so, however, the notes above should give you good food for thought when making your decision.

Chapter 2: The Danger of an S-Corp Bonus

When we think about the idea of a bonus, there is almost invariably a positive connotation to it. Bonus bucks, bonus bites, and if you're really fortunate a bonus from your employer. They're a prize – and all for no additional cost. Yippee!

Some companies have even made a science of creating the *illusion* of a bonus – such as Jos. A. Bank's preposterous "Buy 1, Get **7** Free" and similar deals. A true bonus? Well, maybe not so much.

There is however at least one instance when an honest-to-goodness bonus is a <u>bad</u> idea.

Let's say that your business has enough income to lead you to the conclusion that it should be taxed as an S-Corporation. When I'm meeting with prospective clients or talking to existing clients I seem to get one question more than any other: "How do I pay myself if I need more money than my salary? A bonus?"

Again, the major advantage to the S-Corporation is that earnings in excess of officer **payroll earnings** are not subject to self-employment (Social Security and Medicare) taxes. Business owners must give themselves a reasonable salary, as required by the IRS.

And that often leads to the question: "how do I pay myself if I need more money?" The initial inclination (a bonus) is actually the worst option. Bonuses have to be run through payroll and are de facto employee earnings. As such, they will still be subject to Social Security and Medicare taxes – thus negating the benefit of the S-Corporation.

Instead, corporate shareholders need to take these cash withdrawals as **shareholder distributions.** These can also be called owner withdrawals, stockholder draws, or dividends. Structured in this way, none of these cash withdrawals are subject to SS and Medicare. The income from an S-Corporation is taxed when earned, not when distributed. So there is no additional tax paid for simply withdrawing money from the S-Corp. Income tax was already assessed when the income was earned.

So the basic rule of thumb is: salary to an appropriate and reasonable amount and anything beyond that as a shareholder distribution. There are very few instances where an owner bonus would be appropriate. And again, to be clear, I'm not saying that you as the owner should not pay yourself out the money. You're getting the exact same amount. It's just a question of classifying in the most tax-advantaged manner possible – so that you get to keep more of what you take out instead of having it make that one-way trip to Washington, DC.

Chapter 3: Cash Flow Management / What If I Forget the Books?

Ted: What if I don't think of the books?
Robin: Excuse me?
Ted: There's this famous architecture story about this architect who designed this library. It was perfect. But every year, the whole thing would sink a couple inches into the ground. Eventually the building was condemned. ...He forgot to account for the weight of the books. This company...it's just me. What if I don't think of the books?

In this conversation between two of the main characters in *How I Met Your Mother*, Ted Mosby worries about the future of his fledgling architecture firm. The story he cites has proven to be urban legend, but it does illustrate an interesting point: the most elementary things can sometimes escape us. The simplest mistake can "sink the library" as it were.

The areas where this can happen are frighteningly prevalent. A misunderstanding of tax law or mistakes in tax filings can cost a company thousands and thousands of dollars. Poor hiring decisions can haunt a company for years. The examples are too numerous to even list. But there is one area that affects every business regardless of size, location, or industry.

Cash (by "cash" I'm not talking about actual paper money. Cash as a business term means liquid funds in a bank account or money market fund that are available for use by the business). No matter how much we love what we do, we are in business to make a profit. Without profits a business cannot survive of course, and unless one is independently wealthy, we business owners cannot continue in our chosen field or craft – no matter how fulfilling we might find them. At the end of the day, this is what business is all about.

Very closely related to profits in a business is the <u>critical matter of cash flow.</u> The two are related, but are not exactly the same thing. As an example, think of someone who owns a business buying and selling rare baseball cards. Perhaps that business buys an inventory of these collectible cards and two years later their value has risen dramatically. A great profit! Successful business, right?

Hmm…but what if the business didn't have enough cash on hand or day-to-day sales coming in to pay rent, employee salaries, etc. while waiting for those lovely baseball cards to go up in value and be sold for a profit? The business could be forced to close prematurely and never get to achieve those profits.

CASH FLOW – <u>it is the fuel that powers the engine of businesses and allows them to reach profitability</u>. And yet, proper cash flow planning remains one of the most overlooked and under-planned aspects of many businesses.

Fifty percent of small businesses fail within the first five years. Fifty percent. And it is not because the business owners do not work hard or know their industry. It is often because they forget "the books" – usually involving a miscalculation regarding their cash flow.

This is one of the things I consistently see with small businesses. Good ideas, great craftsmen – but they have failed to do a thorough budget or cash flow projection. And if they have failed to do this, expenses are seriously underestimated or future revenue considerably overestimated. Business owners assume employees will be productive 100% of the time. They forget about unemployment taxes, workers' comp, and the employer half of FICA taxes when calculating the cost of hiring an employee. They might forget about the cost of different insurances they have to carry or that many utility companies require a 3+ month deposit when service is switched. Software upgrades, equipment purchases, vehicle gas getting to jobs, and general office supplies are not properly accounted for. And virtually **everyone** assumes that their services will be more in demand in the beginning than is the reality. And they further assume that demand will grow faster than it truly will.

None of these are unforgivable sins. Heck – some are even natural. We believe we provide the best service/product and at the best price. Why *wouldn't* people be flocking to us from the very beginning? And we are absolutely delightful people – **of course** our employees are going to work hard for us! And the other expenses are easy to let slip through the cracks when we are planning.

But if you combine a few of those things together, you have a company that is **severely** cash strapped, illiquid, and in danger of going under. All of which could have been avoided with some simple planning at the outset. That is why I always advise businesses to create a comprehensive budget and cash flow projection before undertaking any venture. The relatively small cost of the service will pay you dividends for years to come. It may even save your business from avoidable catastrophe.

Chapter 4: Has Your Business Borrowed Too Much? How to Measure and Manage Your Business Debt for Better Cash Flow

"Debt is the slavery of the free." – Publilius Syrus

I'm a firm believer that every business can benefit from a certain amount of debt. Borrowing fuels growth, can get you through lean months, and actually increases some measures of profitability.

Too much of a good thing, of course, leads to trouble. So how much is too much?

There are several ways to find out if your business is "over leveraged", including simple financial measures of your company performance, looking at cash flow, and consulting with a pro.

1. Do the Math

Let's first look at 3 simple math formulas (financial ratios) that are helpful indicators:

- **Debt to Asset Ratio = (Total Debt / Total Assets)**

- The debt to asset ratio shows how much you have borrowed compared to how much you own. This ratio should be below 40% in most industries.
- **Debt to Income Ratio = (Annual Debt Payments / Total Income)**
- The debt to income ratio shows how much of your income is eaten up by debt repayments and this ratio should also be below 40%.
- **Acid-Test Ratio = [(Current Assets – Inventory) / Current Liabilities]**
- The acid-test ratio measures how easily you could pay off your current debts. Ideally this should be 1 or greater.
- Again, the target values are **general** suggestions. Your industry changes what is considered normal or healthy, but these are all good baseline figures.

2. When You Have No Cash

Poor cash flow is another symptom of an over-leveraged company. If your income statement shows that you have reasonably high profits, but you never seem to have much cash on hand, then you may have too much debt. For instance, imagine your company had $200,000 in profit last year. That much money should eventually show up in your checking account, right? Not necessarily.

Paying off debt is **not** an "expense" – just a transfer between two accounts – so paying back principal on loans is not reflected in the $200,000 profit figure. Other things that decrease your available cash but do not reduce profit include paying income taxes, taking owner withdrawals, and investing in assets like cars or buildings (before depreciation). These factors can easily eat up any cash you might have generated from profits.

So what can be done to correct a bad cash flow? The answer varies based on your situation, but there are several areas to examine:

- **Reduce non-critical staff** (which can mean the owner takes on more of the work!) This is most helpful when sales cycles are long and the business is lagging behind competitors in its costs or pricing. Just be sure the cuts are not going to endanger customer relationships or cause other costs.
- **Hire more salespeople** and structure their compensation to be highly commission based. This works well when the business simply needs more revenue to pull itself out of a hole.
- **Don't reduce debt.** Counter-intuitively, paying off debt might make the situation worse before it gets any better. Sometimes it is better to **pay the debt more slowly** and allow the cash flow time to recover. In the end, of course, getting the debt under control is the goal but if it is accelerated to the point that the company is illiquid and unable to continue operations, what is the point?

3. Get Advice

When too much debt is threatening your company there are four pieces of advice that will hold true in all situations.

- **Do Not Ignore Taxes.** If you fall behind on tax payments, the IRS will find out, will probably assess penalties and interest, and may prosecute if they believe you committed fraud. Contact them, inform them of the situation, and attempt to set up a payment plan that fits your budget.
- **Prioritize Loan Repayment.** Start by repaying your highest interest loans. Try to use the capital raised from overhead reduction or revenue increases to pay off the debt to help ensure that there will not be a cash flow issue in the future.
- **Examine Your Lifestyle.** In many situations, getting the business back on track requires that you (the business owner!) live on less personally and leave more cash in the business. Is your business supporting you beyond your means? When you are the boss you have to take the good with the bad. Cut back in the short term to grow a larger, more sustainable business that will continue to support you in the long-term.
- **Consult a Professional.** Just do it. Every situation is different. A few hours of discussion with a qualified professional before a major decision or shift in corporate strategy could very well save your business. Being "frugal" (read: cheap) in this matter and trying to do everything yourself is seldom prudent. I have seen countless companies suffer from payroll penalties, mistakes in tax returns, and operational inefficiencies that could have paid for my fees many times over. And the value of hiring qualified help is not isolated to accountants. Find

someone with the right credentials for your company's situation and hire them for a few hours a month on an ongoing basis, or at least when major decisions are being made.

Having too much debt can be a daunting problem. Focus on the light at the end of the tunnel. When the debt is paid off (or at least reduced to a reasonable level), the business will not suffer the constant struggle of cash flow and high interest expense. It will allow you to focus on actual management of the company and its growth – much more fun than just trying to reduce costs. A sustainable business can grow without the fear of one small mistake sinking the company. And when your business is on solid ground, life is good – at least some of that entrepreneurial stress will melt away!

So act now! Do not wait to act on something that will make your life better and your company more successful. Admitting there is a problem is the first step. Actually doing something about it is the second step that so few people actually take. Get the help you need to give you and your business a brighter future.

Chapter 5: In All Things Balance

"Necessity is not an established fact, but an interpretation" –
Friedrich Nietzsche

I love my job. As dry as accounting seems, I find it fascinating. You get insight into a business's operations and finances – truly the core of what is going on. People open up to you on things they would not with someone who is not a financial professional. You get a view into their lives that few other people are allowed.

And this insight goes beyond simply the core of finances. As you discuss with people the best way to approach their issue, you start to find out about their lives in general. And in these discussions various psychological perspectives on money become apparent. As noted in the debt section above, sometimes business owners are less inclined to tighten their belts than called for when times get tough. On the other hand, some people go to the other extreme of cost reduction – possibly to their detriment. It seems that few people fully understand what **necessity** truly is.

To illustrate these two mindsets I have invented two of the lamest superheroes in history: Captain Penny Pincher and Excessive Spending Man.

Captain Penny Pincher

All right, this guy is fairly obvious. Things are bad or start to go downhill financially and he cuts spending. He cuts anywhere and everywhere he can to get rid of so-called "fat". Most accountants love this guy. I hate him. Why?

One of my bigger issues with other accountants in general is that they just look at the bottom line and try to "reduce costs, reduce costs, reduce costs". That's great – to a point. But what Captain Penny Pincher and these accountants fail to consider is this: "saving" money can easily cost you money.

What do I mean? In the majority of cases you are getting **something** for the money you spend. The key is to figure out if you are getting an adequate return on each expenditure. When a business goes downhill, some people start to indiscriminately slash and burn their budgets. They close down offices, cut staff, reduce advertising, stop traveling to visit clients, and start doing every task themselves. Then they are very proud because they saved $60,000.

The sounds good on the surface, but what was given up? For example, let's say they closed one location and laid off the office person there, but then they lost $80,000 worth of business because the customers left. That $60,000 in reduced expenses ended up reducing their income by $20,000. And all of their time is spent on menial tasks instead of managing the business, which further hurts them. All in the name of "saving" money.

Excessive Spending Man

ESM (as he is commonly known since he is a household brand as of this book) operates in the opposite fashion. And while both habits can be equally detrimental, Excessive Spending Man's refusal to recognize/try to correct the situation makes it even less forgivable. He can't seem to stand reducing personal spending, no matter how lavish it may be. He "needs" his Starbucks every morning. He "needs" to go eat fancy dinners every night. He "needs" to take trips to Cabo every month. And the business operates just as it has – even if it is losing money or has consistently negative cash flow.

The positive thing about ESM is that he is not afraid to spend money where he needs to. The unfortunate part is that he refuses to eliminate spending in the areas he does not. In personal life there are numerous ways to live more simply. And in the business there *are* areas that need to be cut. Sometimes staff members do need to be let go – either based on their performance or the number of people doing a job. Some overhead costs are excessively high. Some forms of advertising simply are not cost effective. ESM bemoans the state of his company but refuses to get the help he needs to correct the issues.

"In All Things Balance"

My Dad said that phrase to me so many times growing up that I assumed it was a quote, scripture, or African proverb. It wasn't – it was just something he said. But no other piece of advice has ever held so true in **every** situation I have encountered. And it holds true here.

You cannot go around cutting every expense possible. It ends up being a "penny wise and pound foolish" approach. There is a quote from Henry Ford I have always loved: *"[a] man who stops advertising to save money is like a man who stops a clock to save time."* Revenues in a business are not where they need to be and most people immediately do not want to spend money on advertising. What sense does that make? Spend smartly and effectively, but **spend**! This is a concept that is beyond the comprehension of most "bean counter" CPAs.

There are a number of free and low cost advertising methods available – especially in the digital space. I always recommend effective internet search engine optimization (SEO) work. While it should not be the only form of advertising a company uses, in my experience it has the highest ROI (return on investment) and should certainly be the first.

If you truly do not have enough work, then you have no reason to hire help. Most people do not go out cold calling with the extra five hours a day they have but instead usually just sit around twiddling their thumbs. But once things get busier, business owners need to consider what areas of responsibility to relinquish. Do you as an owner really need to be doing basic administrative duties when you could be performing services, maintaining customer relationships, or drumming up new clients? At a certain point it makes sense to get rid of some of these duties so you can focus on managing your actual business.

The examples of areas to continue (or start) spending money are countless. But at the same time business owners need to be cognizant of the reality of their business and their own personal habits. In down periods, things *do* need to be cut. The crucial point is to find out which areas are providing the least value and eliminating them. And personal spending must go down or else the business will be bled dry. But if all of this is not done strategically, these changes can do more harm than good.

Chapter 6: The True Cost of the Home Office Deduction

Most of my clients know that I am not a big fan of the home office deduction *especially* if they are homeowners. While it is certainly tempting to be able to deduct a portion of your otherwise non-deductible personal expenses, in most cases it is simply not worth the cost. I'll break this into four sections, **with the fourth being the least advertised but the most important**.

Increase of Audit Risk

The most well-known issue is the fact that taking the home office deduction greatly increases your chances of being audited. People often try to take the deduction in situations where they should not rightfully be doing so and it is a huge red flag to the IRS. The IRS has had great success in disallowing these deductions and continues to look more closely at taxpayers who attempt to take it.

Most of the Expenses are Deductible Elsewhere

If you are a homeowner then your mortgage interest, PMI (usually), and real estate taxes are already deductible on your Schedule A. By claiming the home office deduction you are simply *moving* a portion of those expenses to Form 8829. The only extra expenses you are allowed are a percentage of your home utilities and some depreciation on your home. As we will highlight later, those deductions often end up being comparatively inconsequential.

High Chance of the Deduction Being Disallowed

The IRS has been effective in disallowing this deduction as many taxpayers are not able to meet the two main tests of:

1. Regular and exclusive use
2. Principal place of business

Oftentimes the IRS finds that the office space is also used for personal things or that it is not truly the principal place of business. The latter was the case in *Xiong v. Commissioner, T.C. Summ. Op. 2007-96.* In that case, the IRS disallowed the deduction taken by Texas A&M professor Jin Xiong while he was publishing a book – which was not paid for by the university nor a condition of his employment with the it. The court noted:

*"Petitioner has not convinced us that his book writing project is a **separate activity rather than an outgrowth of his university teaching and research**. While it may be true, as petitioner suggests, that university professors generally are not required to write books, it does not follow that a university professor who writes a book is engaged in a separate business activity. Petitioner's book is in the **same academic discipline as the one petitioner teaches at the university**. Petitioner's contract with Cambridge University Press clearly identifies petitioner as a*

*university professor. Petitioner based his book, at least in part, on teaching notes he had developed over the years, and he used the book in teaching courses at the university. We find that petitioner's book writing project is **so interconnected with his university teaching and research as to not constitute an activity separate from that of his occupation as a university professor**."*

The professor admittedly had some missteps:

- The book would later be used as a course book in his classes at Texas A&M, which linked it to his work as a professor
- He took the deduction in years he had no income from the book
- He claimed he could not use his Texas A&M office for writing but offered no evidence to substantiate this
- He did not show that the office was for his employer's (the publisher) convenience rather than his own
- The list goes on

But what it does highlight is that even if the employer is different and the work not inherently related to existing employment, the IRS can easily make the connection. If the self-employment or secondary occupation is very closely related to existing employment where you already have an office, the IRS could reasonably make the link and disallow it. That does not even factor in the other factors that could cause the deduction to be disallowed. The chart below helps walk people through the decision:

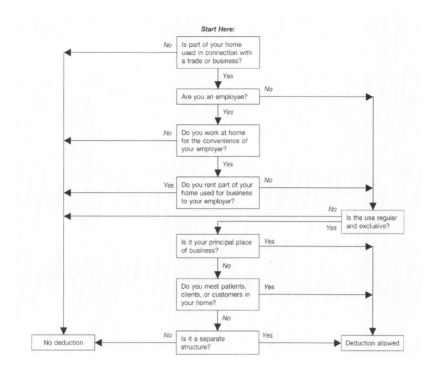

Is part of your home used in connection with a trade or business?

No

Yes

Are you an employee?

No

Yes

Do you work at home for the convenience of your employer?

No

Yes

Do you rent part of your home used for business to your employer?

Yes

No

Is the use regular and exclusive?

No

Yes

Is it your principal place of business?

Yes

No

Do you meet patients, clients, or customers in your home?

Yes

No

Is it a separate structure?

No

Yes

No deduction

Deduction allowed

Increasing Taxable Income in the Future

Now to the most important (and potentially costly) point. If you are a homeowner, the deduction could make your tax bill skyrocket once you sell your home. There are two key points to look at:

1. The possibility of a taxable gain
2. Depreciation recapture

1. If your office is a **separate structure** from the rest of your house, then the gain may very well be taxable (see Pub 587). In those cases you are essentially telling the IRS, "this space is not my home/residence – this is an office used in business." Why is this important? Because gains of less than $250,000 for single taxpayers or $500,000 for married taxpayers on a home that was a principal residence two of the last five years are **tax free**. But if you claim that the separate structure was not truly a residence, *that* portion of the gain is **taxable**.

To illustrate, let's say that 15% of your home expenses are related to this separate structure and it is claimed as an office and you have a $100,000 gain on the sale. That means that the gain on that 15% of the home is taxable – a $15,000 increase in taxable income. The majority of the expenses were already deductible on Schedule A. The only benefit you got was temporary depreciation (see below) and 15% of your utility bills every year. That "deduction" just increased your tax bill far more than it ever reduced it.

Please note: this no longer relates to offices that are physically part of your house. Per Pub 523: *"If the part of your property used for business or to produce rental income is within your home, such as a room used as a home office for a business, you do not need to allocate gain on the sale of the property between the business part of the property and the part used as a home."*

2. Even if your office is a part of your home, the depreciation has be recognized as an unrecaptured section 1250 gain. Note that choosing not to take the depreciation does not give any benefit. Per the IRS: *"If you do not claim depreciation on that part of your home that is a home office, you are still required to reduce the basis of your home for the **allowable** depreciation of that part of your home that is a home office when reporting the sale of your home."* Essentially, if you could have taken it then IRS acts as though you did when calculating your gain. This can only be avoided by using the simplified home office deduction option announced January 2013, but this is capped at $1,500 and 300 square feet per year.

Bottom line: if you are a renter, are not deterred by the never-ending hassles, and truly meet all of the requirements to take the home office deduction then by all means do so. The risks you take are the chance of audit and the deductions potentially being disallowed. But if you are a homeowner, think long and hard about the **true** cost of taking this deduction.

Chapter 7: Independent Contractor vs. Employee

"A little bit independent in your walk
A little bit independent in your talk

…

A little bit independent with your smile
A little bit independent in your style"
– Fats Waller *"A Little Bit Independent"*

With the start of each year, many people start thinking about changes they want to make. Losing weight, home projects, and for business owners – the direction of their businesses. If business has been growing, you may need to hire additional help. This is exciting and daunting all at the same time. Beyond wages, there are other costs to consider: employee benefits, workers compensation, unemployment and FICA taxes, payroll processing costs – all of these are additional costs that the employer may or will have to face.

Because of this, the temptation for some smaller businesses is to instead classify hired persons as "independent contractors". This can be much easier and eliminates the costs mentioned above. The problem? In many cases, the person is not truly an independent contractor but rather a bona fide employee.

With all due apologies to Fats (see the song above) your new worker is not "a little bit independent" in terms of whether he or she is an independent contractor. Properly assessed, the worker is either a contractor or an employee – not a "little bit" of anything – any more than someone is a "little bit pregnant."

Why does it matter? Well, there are a couple of entities to which this is very important. And they are getting more and more touchy about it and are increasingly focused on making sure that employers handle this matter correctly. Who are these folks? Oh, just a couple of small organizations known as the Internal Revenue Service and the Department of Labor. So yeah, it's a good idea to make sure we're approaching this the right way.

BUT…they haven't made it is easy to figure it out and reach the right conclusion. (It's the government – are you surprised?)

The Difficulty in Finding a Definition

Beyond the temptation to classify all workers as independent contractors, it can get pretty confusing once you actually start digging through the laws. A well intentioned employer can get very different answers from different sources. Here are some quotes from governmental agencies to illustrate (feel free to skim to just the bolded sections):

- *"Whether or not a worker is covered by a particular employment, labor, or tax law hinges on the definition of an employee. **Yet, statutes usually fail to clearly define the term "employee", and no single standard to distinguish between employee and independent contractor has emerged."** – Department of Labor*

- *"The Supreme Court has said that **there is no definition that solves all problems relating to the employer-employee relationship** under the Fair Labor Standards Act (FLSA). The Court has also said that determination of the relation cannot be based on isolated factors or upon a single characteristic, but depends upon the circumstances of the whole activity." – Department of Labor*

- *"The Internal Revenue Service developed a list of **20 factors** that may be examined in determining whether an employer-employee relationship exists. The **degree of importance of each factor varies** depending on the occupation and the factual context in which the services are performed; **factors other than the listed 20 factors may also be relevant**." – Internal Revenue Service*

- *"A test is used in most states to determine status under workers' compensation laws. The so- called "economic realities test" or a **hybrid** of the right-to-control and economic realities test often is used by courts to determine independent contractor status in other circumstances." – Department of Labor*

Confused yet? "No definition, "20 factors" and then some more, "importance varies", "hybrid" – no wonder business owners do not know what to do!

Most Important Factors

Given the complexity of the issue, I would be remiss if I tried to comprehensively cover the subject in one article. First, as outlined above, no one article could ever fully capture all of the factors involved. Second, even if I tried, the article would be so long that it would put you to sleep. But here are **quick** descriptions of a few of the **most** key factors that the courts have taken into consideration:

1. Degree of control the employer has/degree of independence the worker has
2. Skill level required for the job
3. Permanency of relationship
4. Worker's opportunities for profit/loss
5. Amount of worker's investment in facilities/equipment
6. How integral the worker's efforts are to the company

Again, those are just short blurbs on a very few of the many, sometimes conflicting parameters that are set out. What if a worker has little independence but a lot of investment in their own facilities and equipment? A long relationship but not integral to the company? Mix in those factors along with the 20+ from the IRS and it can become overwhelming.

Conclusion

As with the choice of corporate setup in the first section, this may be one area where hiring a professional for some advice is beneficial. If you are cautious, the temptation upon reading this might be to retreat in fear and automatically call everyone an employee – just the be safe. But if it's not necessary to do so, you might be costing your business unnecessarily. Incorrect worker classification **in either direction** can be a very costly mistake.

Chapter 8: Inventory Timing and How It Can Affect Your Taxes

"An accountant is someone who solves a problem you didn't know you had in a way you don't understand."

OK, that old line, as with many jokes, contains a certain amount of truth. You're a business owner and you're an expert in your particular field. You're not supposed to know the intricacies of accounting and taxes. So yeah, there can be "problems you didn't know you had" and to be sure, that's where accountants come in. But solving it "in a way you don't understand"? I'm not sure that's the wisest approach. Do you need to become an accounting expert? Of course not. Again, that's your CPA's job. But I do think that it's healthy for you to have a general understanding of what problems can exist, and ultimately how your advisors can best solve them for you. (I'll expand on this in a later section).

I don't usually write "Accounting 101" type articles. As you've seen in this publication, normally I focus on the tax code, business strategy, and other things in that same vein. But based on some business tax returns I've seen recently I thought it might be good to write a few articles focused on some key accounting principles that can have a huge effect on a company's profit and loss in a given year. If you have at least a decent working knowledge of these matters, it becomes a relatively easy process for us together to plan around them accordingly. If you don't have this basic understanding you can find yourself with unexpected pain come tax season.

And keep in mind, these are not comprehensive or exhaustive discussions of the intricacies of accounting. Trust me, you probably wouldn't want me to write anything that long or detailed (unless you happened to be suffering from insomnia, in which case an in-depth treatise on business accounting would probably be just what you needed). Instead, these quick recaps will simply serve as an effective "heads-up" about certain important issues and will help you to see whether a more serious look into your business accounting practices are needed.

In this first section I'm going to talk about inventory timing.

Year End Inventory and Cost of Goods Sold

Constantly keeping track of inventory is a pain. Unless you are a retail operation and keep up with specific items for reordering purposes or are a company that bills material costs back to the customer, many people just put the entirety of a purchase straight into Cost of Goods Sold (COGS).

And for a lot of small or incidental items, this can make practical sense. No one wants to put 100 $1.00 widgets into inventory as separate items and then reduce the inventory count one at a time each time you sell one for $2. For small businesses, and in particular for small dollar and small quantity inventory items, there is the assumption that these will be used in short order and the purchase just goes straight to COGS.

The only issue with this is the **tax** calculation for COGS and how this can impact larger inventory purchases. For tax purposes COGS is calculated in this way on an annual basis:

Beginning of Year Inventory
Plus: Purchases
Less: End of Year Inventory
Equals: COGS

Really, that makes sense if you think about it; it is Cost of Goods **SOLD** after all. Inventory is an asset and shouldn't be expensed until used. If your inventory stayed constant and level year to year this would be fine. But think about a scenario where a company started the year with $10,000 of inventory, had purchases throughout the year of $300,000, and ended with $40,000 in inventory:

Beginning of Year Inventory	$10,000
Plus: Purchases	$300,000
Less: End of Year Inventory	$40,000
Equals: COGS	$270,000

This company legitimately spent $300,000 throughout the year (and has the lack of cash on hand to prove it) but is only getting $270,000 of expense when tallying taxable profits. That could easily be an additional **$10,000** in taxes they did not plan for – for this tax year at least.

This of course swings both ways. If we reverse the beginning and ending inventory the above scenario then the company had COGS of $330,000 for the year. *Theoretically* and over time this all evens out. But year to year it has the potential to wreak havoc on a company's profit and loss.

Furthermore, extremely large swings in a given year could potentially move the company's profits into a higher tax bracket due to an artificially overstated profit in that year, something that might not balance out next year.

Keeping this principal in mind when doing your tax planning will save you a lot of grief come April 15h.

In the next section I'll talk about an equally riveting (*cough cough*) but important topic: accrual vs. cash accounting. Like inventory and COGS, differences in timing can make a huge difference in your tax bill year to year. Stay tuned.

Chapter 9: Accrual Basis vs. Cash Basis Accounting

Q: If an accountant's wife can't get to sleep, what does she say?
A: "Tell me about work today, dear."

Welcome to Round 2 of *Micah's Accounting 101* (absolutely fascinating stuff, I know). A similar phenomenon to inventory timing can occur based on the whether a business uses "cash basis accounting" or "accrual basis accounting". As with inventory accounting, theoretically and over time these differences even out, but <u>timing differences</u> can cause unexpected issues.

Cash Basis Accounting

First, what is cash basis accounting and what is accrual basis accounting? What's the difference between the two? Cash basis accounting is simple: when you receive money you recognize it as revenue and when you spend it you recognize it as an expense. Money in equals sales. Money out equals an expenditure (assuming it actually was a business expense, of course).

Accrual Basis Accounting

Accrual basis accounting is a little different. Under accrual accounting, income is recognized when it is **earned** and expenses are recognized when they are **incurred**. The actual date of the receipt or disbursement of cash is not taken into consideration.

Throughout the year this doesn't make a ton of difference. You receive a bill in January and pay it in February or a customer pays you in April for an invoice you sent out in March. Who cares? But variances towards the beginning or the end of the year can affect your tax return.

For instance, let's say you are an accrual basis company and send out a number of invoices totaling $20,000 on December 31. There is no chance that you will receive that money before the year is done, but by virtue of invoicing (and thus demonstrating that you have earned the income), the entirety of that $20,000 is taxable in the current year. If you were having a bad income year to begin with, you probably don't mind. But if you were already having a bumper year then the last thing you want is more income! It means the tax is due today vs. a year from now and you're quite possibly paying it **at a higher rate**. More tax and sooner. Not good.

Cash basis is a little more straightforward but it can trip you up as well. If a business were a cash basis company and invoiced out late in 2014, all of the income is taxable when received in 2015. You might predict this for a December 31 invoice, but what about an invoice from September that a customer doesn't get around to paying you until February? Since the payment was so late, you might have forgotten it was income for the current year.

None of this is overly difficult to cope with, but it does take appropriate planning. If you just use your bank balance as a barometer for your taxes, *you could be in for a world of hurt come Tax Day.*

Section 2: Marketing & Branding

Chapter 10: Branding and Perception: The Mademoiselle Noir Effect

A couple of years back I stumbled on an interesting song called "Mademoiselle Noir."

The whole premise is the same as Rapunzel (girl in a tower, long hair, etc.) except instead of being viewed as virtuous and lovely, the townspeople think she is evil and fear her.

This isn't the first time a classic story has been retold with a drastically different slant. There seem to be a lot of tales that are being retold from an alternate viewpoint. (An example being the hit Broadway show "Wicked" which cast the Witch of the West as the heroine/protagonist). These stories often make you sympathize with the "villain" and root against the "hero" – at least as they were structured in the original telling.

This highlights just how important perspective is. Substance is important. It actually is the single most important thing when you are a practitioner of any craft. But substance without the corresponding *perception* of substance is useless for a small business owner.

How could we be hurting ourselves in this regard? Well, consider the following scenarios with people's vehicles:

- A financial advisor who drives a $1,000 jalopy
- A mechanic whose car is appears in disrepair and often breaks down
- A construction professional who drives out to bid jobs in a tiny Miata

Be honest, how good do you think any of those people are at their jobs? Why can't the financial manager afford something better for himself; why would a mechanic not be able to fix his own car; and what kind of serious construction company exec has a car the size of a coffee table?

In truth, there might be plausible reasons for all of these situations:

- The financial advisor has 8 kids and takes care of his parents (and knows that cars are lousy investments!)
- The mechanic's car has sentimental value and the mechanic keeps it despite its fundamental problems
- The car is on loan from a friend while the F350 pickup truck is in the shop

But did you as the consumer know that? Would you have thought that? Or did you do what is natural in human nature and question their abilities? Chances are you would have.

That is why it's important for us as business owners to take careful stock of our image. Are we perceived in the way that we want to be perceived? Are we projecting to the customer the value that we know we have?

If we aren't, we need to correct this. Sometimes it costs money to do so. But we can't ignore the problem because things are difficult. We have to take careful stock of what it costs us not to fix it (in terms of lost revenues, referrals, etc.) Tennis great Andre Agassi was famously cast in a commercial in which he stated "image is everything." It's not *everything* in business – since no amount of image polishing makes up for lack of quality or expertise – but an image that properly creates the desired impression and customer perception is certainly not an irrelevant afterthought either.

Chapter 11: The Market Will Not Bear Generalists

I once knew someone that claimed that he could coach companies to make more profit. Fantastic. But I could never get him to tell me what he *actually* did. I spoke with him multiple times, read his entire website, and looked at all of his posts online **just** to try to figure out what the service really was. To this day I still have no idea. Nothing that was ever said truly meant anything. Everything was some combination of vague non-statements and clichés:

- "Run your business more efficiently"
- "Keep more of your profit"
- "Increase revenue"
- "Reduce expenses"
- "Get more organized"

At a certain point I expected "buy low and sell high" and "a rolling stone gathers no moss" to be thrown in there. Sure they were good goals to have, but they didn't *mean* anything. They didn't tell you what he did, what value he was ostensibly providing, and how this would benefit your company.

But in every sentence he managed to throw in some variation of "make more profit." It reminded me of an old episode of the show *South Park*. In the admittedly ridiculous storyline, a group of gnomes went around stealing underpants from people's dressers. When asked why, they invariably screamed "profit!" It was later revealed that this was their business model:

Phase 1	Phase 2	Phase 3
Collect Underpants	?	Profit

Why am I even telling this story?

As small business owners, we are often operating in a very competitive environment. People are reluctant to spend any money and when they finally decide to they have a plethora of options. For any of us to succeed, we have to be **specific** and **focused** as to what we provide. In my mind, these are two related yet separate things.

Specific

The failure in the above example was obviously that nothing was clear. What was the service? What benefits would be derived from it and how? Why was it better than that of competitors? We need to make these things abundantly clear to clients and potential clients. Otherwise our pitch becomes nebulous and unappealing.

Focused

Even if we clearly showcase to clients the things above we still run a certain risk: trying too hard to do too many things. The phrase "jack of all trades" existed before "master of none" was tacked onto the end of it. If we try to be generalists and perform too many services, then we may lose credibility as to what we can *actually* do.

For instance, I'm an accountant. You would believe that I can do taxes, bookkeeping, and some other related services, right? But what if I also said that I could advise you on stocks and other financial matters? And then said that I could get you insurance policies? Also, that I had a realtor's license and could sell your house for you? That I also could do your electrical work in your house? Perform veterinary surgery on your dog? At what point do you start wondering if can do **any** of those things well?

Bottom line: while not being overly limited in our services, we always want to stick to and advertise the areas in which we are truly experts. And when those are determined, we need to make sure those skills are clearly and effectively communicated to those we are doing business with.

Chapter 12: Do Not Become Overly Specific

We've established the pitfalls of being too broad and general in the services we offer – the "Jack of all trades, master of none" phenomenon. However, a danger exists at the other end of the spectrum, so it seems appropriate to write at least a short note on the opposite risk: being overly specific in our skills.

This was something that always struck me when I worked as a financial/business analyst at a large company years ago. In other departments, there were people who were absolute masters of their crafts. Hardworking, intelligent, dedicated, and very knowledgeable. But some of the jobs were so specific that they would have been completely useless in any other industry – sometimes even useless at another company in the very same business!

Obviously someone needed to do those things, otherwise the positions would not have been available – the same as in any other industry. But it does beg the question: do **you** personally want to be a person (or business owner) whose fate and entire area of expertise are tied to one skill, industry, or company? Especially in a world as fast changing as ours?

It reminds me of an episode of the show *30 Rock* in which Liz Lemon (the talented Tina Fey), a TV writer, was afraid her industry was dying in the wake of reality TV shows. She had the following conversation in a dream:

Liz: Who are you?
Woman: Better to ask who we used to be. People whose professions are no longer a thing. Once I was called "Travel Agent".
Man 1: I was an American auto worker.
Man 2: And I played dynamite saxophone solos in rock and roll songs!
Woman: Come [with us]. We live under the subways with the CEO of Friendster.

What will happen to us when the industry or economy shifts? If our industry goes through a turbulent time, do we have a skill set that transfers to another? If technology automates a process, does our knowledgebase still provide us with security? What will we do when the unexpected happens?

If we build a reasonably (but not overly) broad, flexible, and transferable skill set then we are setting ourselves up for success. If we have decided to become the world's greatest switchboard operator, laser disk designer, or telegraph technician then we are not. While still focusing our attention on a select few areas of expertise, we all want to make sure that these skills are not overly specific in case the market, our industry, or our personal circumstances shift.

I have kept this in mind as I have structured my accounting firm. While not being "all things to everyone" I have developed expertise in a wide enough range of financial areas so as to be able to properly address the needs of our small business and individual clients.

I could say (as discussed in the previous chapter) "We do it all! Your taxes, your books, your investments, your home purchase, your lawn, your car, and your dentistry." And we would end up providing lousy service in all those areas.

Or I could say "If you need someone to advise you on the intricacies of the deprecation of mining equipment as it relates to IRS Code Section XYZ paragraph 2 line 6 with regard to foreign subsidiaries then I'm your guy!"

Instead, my firm provides expert service in a <u>few</u> key areas that are needed by and applicable to the needs of a <u>wide</u> group of clients.

Not too broad and not too narrow. The "Goldilocks" approach – not too hot, and not too cold – instead, "just right." That's the sweet spot every company should strive to hit.

Chapter 13: The Empty Box Phenomenon

My favorite uncle (Sam), has always had a lot of insight. Throughout my life I've often looked to him as a source of perspective and discernment. One of my favorite pieces of advice that he gave actually wasn't directed at me, but to another one of his nephews – John.

As most every other young man has been at one point or another, John was in love. He was hopelessly enamored with a girl who, by all measures, *was* absolutely gorgeous. He asked Sam what he thought about her. Sam's response went something like this:

Sam: Think for a second about how you feel when you get a nice, wrapped gift
John: What do you mean?
Sam: You know, you get the box and it's wrapped in nice, decorative paper. It's covered in ribbons and bows. It looks beautiful and you're just brimming with anticipation to see what's inside
John: Right
Sam: Now think about how you would feel if you got the box, took off the ribbons, ripped off the paper, and there was nothing in there – it was totally empty. Think about how disappointed you would be

John: Sure…

Sam: *laughing* that girl – you've got an empty box right there

I always chuckle when I remember that story, but it has been one that has stuck with me. **Presentation is only as good as the reality of what is inside**. That bit of wisdom from Uncle Sam was dating advice, but it has much broader applications. In our businesses, could we inadvertently become "empty boxes" to our clients and customers?

How might this happen? As I've mentioned before, I believe most of the people I meet and work with are great at what they do. Their craftsmanship and expertise are generally impeccable. But that doesn't always translate into a successful business. And sometimes this has to do with client expectations and how we manage them. I see two errors arise in business operations: 1) overselling or 2) underperforming. I know, both sound so basic you might question why I am even expounding on them. But they can affect us in ways we may not even realize.

Overselling

Is it possible that our presentation (wrapping) is overselling our performance/product (box content)? With everyone, but especially with new clients, we are understandably keen to please. We want to get their business and we want to make our services attractive to them. But what if our pitch is a wee bit *too* attractive?

For instance, I always state my case that I am more affordable than other CPAs, that I give more personal service, and that I provide far superior quality than "bargain" accountants. In my humble opinion, all of that is true. But what if I tried to guarantee that I would save you 90% of the cost of any other CPA firm? Or that you could call me at 3 a.m. to ask me a question and I'd answer, jump out of bed, and come meet you at your office every time? Or that I would save you five times as much on your taxes as a cheapo accountant?

At a certain point, it doesn't matter how well I perform – there is no way I could be remotely close to the unrealistic bar I **unnecessarily** set for myself. While we do not want to be a "Debbie Downer" or be so conservative that there isn't any reason for client to use us or buy our product (confidence *is* important after all), we also want to be reasonable in our promises

Underperforming

I just got through saying that most people are very good at what they do, so how might this happen? There are two possibilities:

1. We get in a hurry and quality suffers
2. We are so focused on other things we do not have the time to adequately commit to each client

The first point does unfortunately happen (a lot, actually), but again – most of the people I deal with personally and professionally have such pride in their work that doesn't happen frequently. The second point though, is where even the most well-intentioned person can get into trouble. I think the prototypical example of this is a contractor trying to juggle jobs. Not wanting to turn down work, they might take 5-10 jobs on at once and try to manage them all simultaneously. This is often only partially successful, customers have to keep calling to see what is going on, and the jobs end up taking longer than expected. Even when the end result is fantastic, no one is **completely** pleased with the process – because of the irritation over perceived broken promises.

For different reasons, the same can happen to any of us. Most of us are trying to grow our businesses. But how would our existing clients feel if we started neglecting them because we were spending so much time trying to court new business? Even if we were not doing sloppy work, if we did not commit adequate time to each client, then the relationship would inevitably suffer.

Conclusion

All of us do well to take stock of how we are presenting ourselves and how we spend our time. If there is a disparity that is too large – either because we promise too much or give too little – our customer satisfaction will decrease and may harm the relationship for the future.

Chapter 14: Promises, Promises – Be Careful How You Charge Your Clients

"It is an immutable law in business that words are words, explanations are explanations, promises are promises – but only performance is reality." – Harold Geneen

The world has always been filled with promises – some good and some bad. Friends and relatives make commitments to us out of the goodness of their hearts. Many acquaintances and business associates will try to guarantee as much as they can and with honest intention. Unfortunately even with the best motives, some of these promises – for one reason or another – are never followed through on.

And some people promise things purely out of greed with no intention of keeping the promises made. Crooked politicians and dishonest business people have become almost synonymous with this type of "pre-broken" promise.

The point being, regardless of people's intentions, promises are often broken or at least not fulfilled. This may be due to some kind of chicanery or it could be due to something that was completely beyond the promisor's control. As Ovid once said, *"everyone's a millionaire where promises are concerned."* Because of this, many people (consumers) have become jaded.

That is why I often caution my business clients against pricing that is heavy on upfront charges. Even if there is no fraud involved, and even if we can and do have the practice of keeping our business promises, large upfront fees can change the tenor of the conversation completely – and end up causing the business to scare away potential customers. To the consumer, the requirement for upfront money smacks of charlatanism and invokes images of a seedy, 1970s mustached used car salesman.

(**SEE NOTE AT THE END** of this section for situations/industries that are legitimate exceptions to this no-upfront-cost rule).

Like most people, I receive calls or emails on a fairly regular basis pitching me some kind of product or service. Even though I do not need them the majority of the time, I try to at least listen. But at the point in the conversation when I hear "$500 deposit", "one year contract", "monthly minimum", or anything of the like – my interest dissipates completely.

Why? Because there are so many people out there promising you big results *if you pay them upfront*. And as outlined below, sometimes this may be justified and necessary. But if the customer perceives it to be unnecessary, then you've probably already lost the sale.

For example, most of my business associates know that I am a big believer in search engine optimization. But just for my own curiosity I like to read the industry publications to have a basic understanding of the theory. One day I stumbled on a site that sells "backlinks" to your site on other sites. I wasn't going to purchase their product regardless, but the links cost **$1-3** apiece and the company requires a **$400 deposit**. Why on earth would you do that? *If* the product is legitimate, the results will speak for themselves. But requiring a huge payment before any services have been rendered just reeks of dishonesty.

And that's why I almost never require a deposit/retainer and advise most of my business clients to do the same when they can. Requiring a deposit, unless it is a special situation or industry where it is necessary, can often give a bad impression. It can may leave a bad taste in the client's mouth and might even cost you the job.

Note: In certain industries or professions the use of a large deposit is necessary and/or standard practice. Construction companies, custom manufacturing businesses, etc. – industries that involve heavy capital outlay to complete an order or project – often by necessity require a large deposit. Attorneys undertaking a project for a client that will involve a significant number of billing hours at the outset frequently require a retainer and work from that – tallying hours against the initial retainer. These are not objectionable practices. For most businesses in other industries though, such arrangements are not necessary or customary, and the points made above in the article stand.

Chapter 15: Effective Networking: Revere vs. Dawes

> *"I am a wandering, bitter shade,*
> *Never of me was a hero made;*
> *Poets have never sung my praise,*
> *Nobody crowned my brow with bays;*
> *And if you ask me the fatal cause,*
> *I answer only, "My name was Dawes"*
> *– "The Midnight Ride of William Dawes" by Helen F. Moore*

Does anyone out there remember that Paul Revere was not the sole rider on April 18, 1775? Anyone? Anyone? Bueller? There were two other men who rode that night, but they have slipped into obscurity. Why?

There are two possible explanations:

1. Revere's immortality was solidified by Longfellow's "Paul Revere's Ride". As illustrated by the poem above, there is very real speculation that Revere was only chosen because his name was easier to rhyme than those of the other men.
2. Revere was the more prominent figure, the most well-known, and the best connected of all of the riders

The first explanation is the most amusing (and likely has some degree of truth to it), but it is far from a complete explanation. It may help explain why Paul Revere is a household name today, but his reputation in his own time laid the foundation.

Although other men arguably did more that night on an individual level, some historians still credit Revere with the mission's success. Why? **Because he was a networking powerhouse**. He was so involved with the community, was such a strong leader, and was so well known that he accomplished what no one else could. His word carried weight and he was a one man communications machine – moving others to action and coordinating many other riders from the towns he passed. Because of his reputation and relative prestige, Revere was also called to write a testimony of what happened that night – not Dawes.

What's the point?

One of the single hardest problems to correct in small businesses is a lack of revenue generation (not enough business). And business owners will often bemoan the lack of business coming through the door. But just as frequently many will not do anything about it.

That just doesn't work. Especially for a new business, building a brand and a following is the biggest struggle. It is also the thing that will sink you if you are not able to do it quickly enough. And yet people will still sit back, market very passively, and wait for the business to come to them.

Again – it just <u>does not</u> work. As we've noted several times already, the success of a business is not exclusively tied to the quality of the goods or services provided. The best craftsmen are often the worst businesspeople. You cannot rely solely on your product for your fledgling company to succeed. When I first started my practice I always said that for each hour I billed out in those early days I spent <u>40 hours</u> marketing – working hard to build a clientele. Networking events, building relationships, social media, cold calling, SEO (search engine optimization), writing blogs, and other more creative ways of branding – I did and still do all of it. And I am thankful to say that it has worked; I now have a thriving practice. But this takes time and effort – and for anyone seeking to establish a business there is often *considerable* amount of lead time involved before one sees the tangible benefit (business, sales, clients, whatever).

So who do we want to be – William Dawes or Paul Revere? We can put in the effort, build a distinct brand, and forge strong relationships. And if we do we will succeed. Or we can rest on our non-existent laurels and find ourselves looking for a job a year later because the business has failed. The choice is entirely up to us.

Section 3: Valuable Miscellany

Chapter 16: Me, Myself, and I: The Self-Employed Perspective

"I try not to kid myself. You know, I don't mind romancing someone else, but to fool yourself is pretty devastating and dangerous." – Bill Veeck

Hermann Göring was by any measure a horrible human being. During the Second World War he was the second in command of the Nazi Party, the architect of much of the structure of Hitler's Germany, and would have been the successor to Hitler. A truly terrible man.

A minor bit of trivia is that he was also an avid collector of art. And his favorite painter was the Dutch master Vermeer. Apparently Hitler had several works by the artist and Göring desperately wanted one for himself. ("Adolf has three. I want one! All the cool kids are getting them.") So in 1942 he finally purchased one of Vermeer's paintings from Dutch art dealer Han van Meegren for the modern day equivalent of about $7M.

When the Germans lost WWII, Göring was arrested and all of his assets were seized. Additionally, the art dealer van Meegren was arrested and charged with **treason** for aiding and abetting an enemy via the sale. Faced with a possible death sentence, van Meegren made a confession. The painting was not a real Vermeer – it was a forgery he himself had created. The charges were dropped and van Meegren became a folk hero in Holland for having pulled one over on the Nazi bigwig.

My favorite part of the story (and the reason I am relating it today) is Göring's reaction when he found out his beloved painting was a fake. One account states that upon hearing the news the Nazi commander *"looked as if for the first time he had discovered there was evil in the world."* How spectacularly ironic is that? This evil man who had been responsible (directly and indirectly) for unspeakable atrocities finally becomes shaken…by a deception related to his favorite painter.

While it is nearly certain that none of us could become as far removed from reality as Göring was, our perspective regarding life, priorities, and even matters of finance and business can easily become skewed. Spending too much time with like-minded people or without any outside advisors at all can cause us to become mentally entrenched.

I think this might be even more of a risk for those of us who own our own businesses. I absolutely love running my own firm – in no small part because of the level of control I have. All successes and failures are mine alone and everything I do has a direct correlation to how the business performs. Additionally (and this is not a minor perk) I do not have to answer to a boss.

One of most people's least favorite parts of corporate America is dealing with their boss and company bureaucracy. Being freed of red tape and layers of approval processes is amazing and is a positive experience in many instances. As our own bosses we are able to make company decisions immediately and decisively without having to convince a less informed individual (i.e. the 'idiot boss" everyone has had at one point or another). But this is not without some danger.

We all like ourselves. We usually think we're pretty smart guys and gals. So of course we are going to think our decisions are the right ones. Especially without disagreeing co-workers, bosses overseeing our work, or really any dissenting voices – it can become very easy for us to listen and view our own opinions as gospel. (We'd could never – even for a moment –be the "idiot boss", right?) To an extent, that confidence is needed. If we constantly second guess ourselves we will never be successful entrepreneurs (a phenomenon sometimes called "paralysis by analysis"). But blindly following one course without taking a step back to objectively analyze our business is a dangerous course. Hermann Göring was one of the most extreme examples of this.

I've mentioned this throughout this book, so you may think I am beginning to sound like a broken record, but we all need outside advisors and opinions to make sure we continue on the right course. People who are not there to make us happy or tickle our ears, but instead can objectively analyze how things are being run.

Chapter 17: *"No need to worry, my accountant handles that"* – The Notorious B.I.G

As noted earlier, I am all about balance. I believe being balanced is probably the single most important key to success. So I want to be clear that the section above is not intended to mean that small business owners should stop trusting their own instincts or become completely uninterested in whole areas of their business. I only mean that they should not rely exclusively on themselves. Seeking **advice** is prudent, but complete detachment and reliance is a danger.

Since I've been in practice I have found that a lot of people have the Biggie Smalls viewpoint on money management. This sounds reasonable in theory. Accountants are financial professionals. The clients have confidence in their accountants' expertise and trust what is being done – often without question.

But what if you have a bad advisor? What if the guidance you are being given is faulty? Even if the advice is good, what happens if the accountant or financial advisor suddenly dies? Do you have any idea what is going on with your finances?

There have been many celebrities who have fallen into this trap. Anyone who trusted Bernie Madoff was in for a rude awakening several years ago. By all reports Terrell Owens was never a big spender (in celebrity terms at least). Unfortunately he was told to make several very ill-advised investments by financial "experts" and ended up playing arena football to try to make ends meet. Nicholas Cage claims that his advisor led him into financial ruin. Since Nic was buying private islands and dinosaur fossils I'm not sure I really believe him completely, but you get the pattern.

Having blind faith – just mindlessly following *anyone* is ill-advised. I know that, and you probably do as well.

But we are equally ill-advised to rely solely on ourselves to handle matters about which we are not well-informed or educated. And we really should not go it alone when we lack the degree of expertise that is called for to properly navigate confusing or technical aspects of our business. Know what is going on, be involved and informed, but continue to seek outside help and perspective.

Caution & Concluding Thoughts

As I read over this book, I'm pretty pleased with the finished product. Still, I cannot help but note one thing: it is not personalized advice nor can it be a substitute for it.

If you are reading this book, you've purchased something to give you business advice for a low price. And I believe this book does that! This a compilation of information gleaned from years of practice and advice given to businesses like yours. If you follow the principles contained here, you will be ahead of the **vast** majority of your peers – and most importantly, your competitors.

However, it is also incomplete, or at least it will be at some point. There will be, figuratively, if not literally, a new chapter tomorrow or the next day, because each new situation or challenge requires a new solution. That is the fascinating, exciting, and sometimes frustrating aspect of business. Nothing stays the same. And even the (insert gratuitous self-back-patting here) extremely valuable information I have shared will need to be updated, and changes in the business environment in general or your business specifically will require fresh strategies.

You will note that I have mentioned trusted advisors, and the value of outside input throughout the book. The poet John Donne famously wrote "No man is an island, entire of itself." Now, Donne wasn't writing about business. But I am. And I echo his sentiment:

we can't do it alone. No matter how talented the quarterback, he still needs the other guys on the team. I am not stressing this as a sales pitch for my own services (I won't lie – if that happens that's fantastic, but that is not my **purpose**). This is true when it comes to legal matters, insurance needs, yes, accounting/tax, and number of other areas of business as well. Don't be an "island." If you embrace the knowledge or others, allowing them to contribute to your success, you will find your business more profitable and your satisfaction in the work you do will skyrocket – since you can focus on the aspects of your business that you love. And if you don't love your chosen endeavor, and if you can't see your way through the challenges to the point that you are making really good money from your business and building wealth from it – then you should do something else. Just get a job working for someone. Business is tough enough and carries with it enough stresses, that it should reward you really, really well – on all levels.

I stress this point because I think it is so fundamentally important, and I will get on my soapbox and shout to the need to enlist trusted advisors to boost you in your quest for continuing success in business. With the advent of the internet there has been a trend toward believing that do-it-yourself (DIY) works in all situations. And sometimes it does – at least in the short-term. The real estate market was great…until it wasn't. The stock market soars and provides a great return…until eventually it doesn't. Something that looked easy – and which certain authors of articles or books would have led you to believe could be successfully done by yourself in just a few minutes a day in your spare time – turned out not to be so easy after all. "You've got a computer – trade stocks on your own!" "This handy-dandy software package lets you do your own taxes!" "Don't be a sucker and pay someone for advice." "Buy a drill and do your own dentistry!" (Oh wait...we wouldn't do that. But we would, and sometimes do, risk our financial security and success by "winging" it ourselves rather than obtaining expert guidance. And just because something looks easy, doesn't mean that it is. (I watch golf on TV and think "That can't be so hard." Maybe I should be a pro golfer, huh?) I'll illustrate this with one last example:

Robert Kiyosaki is regarded, on the internet and the DIY finance community, as a financial expert. He is revered by many and is looked to as a true authority. A guru.

He is also...an idiot. (OK, I should use a disclaimer: he is, in my personal opinion, an idiot. But basically, yeah, he's a clown.) His whole pitch for years was a "failsafe" way to build your real estate empire. It all worked ok for a while – during the "go-go" years of real estate. And then came the housing and real estate crisis and it all came unglued. Oh yeah, that plan of his clearly ended up working very well for all parties involved. (Insert sarcastic tone there.) Then in 2009 (after his "guru" advice has ruined many people financially) he came out with an article claiming that the 401k is "the biggest scam ever". I won't go into the reasons why his argument is incorrect and preposterous – that is another discussion altogether (although I do think that the fact that the article has been deleted by most of the sites that hosted it speaks for itself). But virtually all of his advice is uniform (call it "one size fits all" or "cookie cutter"), vague, and oftentimes completely incorrect. And remember, he is a "financial expert".

Not every author or supposed expert espousing a DIY approach is as bad as him. Some of them actually have very good **concepts** behind their theories. But their advice is, by definition, uniform. They are appealing to a mass audience. They have to make it so their advice is general and applies to a majority. There is always a chance that you do not fall into that group.

I really hope you've enjoyed the book and would love to hear your feedback and your experiences after implementing the advice. This books is based on the real world – real people in business and the successes and failures I have seen. As I've said, nothing is a substitute for one-on-one expert advice, and you'll need that along the way. But in the meantime, these dynamic and battle-tested strategies will put you head-and-shoulders above your competition and well on your way to even further success in your business.

Work hard, work smart, keep your eyes, ears, and mind open, have fun, and knock 'em dead!

If you'd like to tell me what you thought of the book or would like to get together to discuss your company's specific needs, you can visit my website at FraimCPA.com or give me a call at (540) 314-0345.

Made in the USA
Middletown, DE
06 July 2018